Monique Cohen was born in Sydney, Australia. Always curious about the emotional realm and the human psyche, she trained as a clinical psychologist and specialised in child and adolescent psychotherapy. During her training, she married and had two enchanting and hilariously entertaining daughters. She also has two adorable labradoodles and a rabbit called Vladimir. She is currently working in her own private practice and thoroughly enjoys, and is enlivened by, her interactions with all her clients.

To Tim and Abi,

"Make and treasure the warm, precious moments"

xoxo

Monique.

Planet Parent

Monique Cohen

Austin Macauley Publishers™
LONDON · CAMBRIDGE · NEW YORK · SHARJAH

Copyright © Monique Cohen 2023

The right of **Monique Cohen** to be identified as author of this work has been asserted by the author in accordance with sections 77 and 78 of the Copyright, Designs and Patents Act 1988.

All rights reserved. No part of this publication may be reproduced, stored in a retrieval system, or transmitted in any form or by any means, electronic, mechanical, photocopying, recording, or otherwise, without the prior permission of the publishers.

Any person who commits any unauthorised act in relation to this publication may be liable to criminal prosecution and civil claims for damages.

A CIP catalogue record for this title is available from the British Library.

ISBN 9781398461192 (Paperback)
ISBN 9781398461208 (ePub e-book)

www.austinmacauley.com

First Published 2023

Austin Macauley Publishers Ltd®
1 Canada Square
Canary Wharf
London
E14 5AA

I dedicate this book to my ever-patient and loving husband, Barry, my two adorable daughters, my beautiful affectionate labradoodles, Hermoine and Raziel, and Vladimir, our rabbit.

Firstly, I'd like to acknowledge Austin Macauley Publishers who had faith in the potential of this book and who took a chance on a new author such as myself. The support, respect and encouragement from their team has been incredible. I'd also like to thank an amazing doctor and wonderful person, Dr Alison Vickers, who encouraged me to write several articles for her community magazine Shire's Children. Her words 'you should make these into a book' was the seed that created Planet Parent. My deepest gratitude to my friend, Sharon Harrison, who has always had the utmost faith and confidence in me and encouraged me to publish this book. She helped me nurture the seed. Thanks to the therapists and clinical supervisors who have influenced my clinical work, especially Dr D W Winnicott (deceased), Dr John Howard, Dr Juliet Harper and Peter Blake. Enormous thanks and respect also goes to my brave and vibrant clients for their creativity, exuberance and playfulness and for giving me the honour of sharing some moments in their world.

Chapter One
Introducing Planet Parent

The time has come! Your baby has arrived. You gaze longingly onto it's face and (sometimes with the help of an epidural) the intense agony of expelling a human life out of your body fades.

The doctor says, "congratulations Mum and Dad, it's a girl!"

My partner and I look around and suddenly realise that he is talking to us… we are Mum and Dad! The sudden wave of responsibility is breath-taking, awesome and terrifying.

Our mushed minds became a mix of thoughts of all the media pictures and societal myths of parenthood being relaxing and 'natural'. Along with the extreme horror stories we had heard of parents not sleeping and being driven to madness by the incessant demands of seemingly ungrateful, cold hearted, soulless children. Of course, these are extremes and most parenting involves a variety of good and not-so-good experiences.

I clearly remember being shell-shocked when I was told that you had to teach a baby to sleep and that even breast feeding was not necessarily an innate ability. In fact, babies sometimes had to be prompted to suck the nipple in the right way.

Somehow, I muddled my way through parenthood. I was trained as a Clinical Psychologist and specialised in Child and Adolescent Psychotherapy but this in no way equipped me for being a parent. It did make it extremely interesting and

exciting to observe my own infant develop as my beautiful daughter went on to illustrate and give evidence for the theorists who I had always felt attuned with and admired. I particularly felt connected to Donald Winnicott's theories (a Paediatrician and Psychoanalyst) which emphasised the importance of play in child development and healing. As fascinating as this was, it did not really help when I found myself crying in the corner in total powerlessness and frustration as I could not get my daughter to sleep.

The 24-hour Tresillian Hotline (staffed by wonderful specialist nurses) was my rock! I sometimes rang it three or four times a night to get reassurance and sometimes to get a variety of nursing opinions if I did not feel comfortable with the first advice.

Often, they would simply say, "You've tried everything there is nothing else you can do."

Strangely, this would be very comforting.

It seemed to highlight the Winnicottian notion that as a parent (or human for that matter) it is impossible to be 'perfect'. The best anyone can strive for is to be 'good enough' most of the time.

This book is a collection of articles written in a humorous manner offering parents knowledge and advice. It is drawn from my training and experience as a child and adolescent psychotherapist of over 30 years and from my hilarious adventures with my own children. The articles were first written for a free local health magazine that was developed by a wonderful local general practitioner, Dr Alison Vickers, with a passion to educate and empower parents.

Topics covered include good enough parenting, self-care,

Fathering, Paternal Post-natal Depression, importance of childhood games, labels, violence in the media, the dilemma of children playing computer games, Perfectionism and the challenge of Gifted children. The book imparts information about childhood development and gives parents/caregivers strategies to better engage with their child and adolescent. Thus, this good connection will hopefully avert some disasters and create a protective shield to help navigate through some of the toxic elements of life in our current world.

Planet Parent is aimed at new parents (although I think any parent would find this helpful and amusing) and it encourages the reader to understand and enjoy their children despite the many challenges of parenthood.

Chapter Two
'Good Enough' Parenting

Parents often put an incredible amount of pressure on themselves to be perfect. This is an impossible endeavour as humans are not perfect. We all have our vulnerabilities and flaws which also empowers us to empathise and show compassion. We love our children, want to do better than what our parents did with us and also give our kids the good experiences that we enjoyed in our childhood. Every child is unique and has a different personality, gift, challenges and life experience. There is no magic google page or book specifically for your child. 'Perfect' parenting is impossible but 'good enough' parenting is very achievable.

Donald Winnicott (Paediatrician, Psychoanalyst) developed the notion of 'good enough' parenting, as the parent's adaptation to the baby, giving it a sense of control and comfort at being connected to the parent. This 'holding environment' lets the child transition at their own rate to be more independent. Winnicott saw that as the physical holding of the baby is important, so too is the emotional holding. 'Good enough' holding involves being able to anticipate and keep the child's needs and desires thoughtfully in mind and placed (as much as possible) as a priority amongst the other demands in life. The parent assists the child to have a healthy sense of independence by moving away from the child in well-timed small measures. The aim is to give the child a sense of the hold appropriately loosening rather than being dropped.

Of course, in order to create a 'good enough' holding environment, it is essential that parents take care of themselves so that they feel 'held' and have the emotional space to deal with the child's needs. Children learn how to self soothe when they are tired or distressed by observing how their parents soothe themselves. By taking care of yourself you are also modelling helpful coping mechanisms to your child.

There are many ways to highlight to your children that you keep them thoughtfully in mind. The following are some important strategies:

- Make it a priority to spend regular one-to-one time with each child in the family. Even one hour a week would be an amazing positive experience, for your child (and hopefully for you too). In that special time, let the child know that you are entirely there for them. Tell them that you won't be answering the phone, texting, on the computer nor doing housework. Try and find a play activity that you both enjoy. Children are amazing little sponges when it comes to picking up your emotions no matter how well you hide it. They will feel it if you're having fun too!

- Try and have regular time and holidays as a nuclear family. Spending time with other relatives and friends is wonderful but it cannot take the place of regular space for time with just Mum and Dad and the children. Children develop their identity and ability to interact with other humans in the world from their attachment and interaction

with their parents and siblings. Having special nuclear family time and holidays is essential and nurtures this development.
- Create family rituals such as family weekly walks, eating dinner together and sharing stories about the day's adventures. Have a regular park that you take the children to on a particular day and be involved in their play. This can be as active as chasing them around the play equipment pretending to be a 'wild squirrel' or simply watching and praising their prowess on the swings.

Good enough parenting develops your child's inner protective armour and nurtures their resilience. At times, when you're exhausted and you feel haunted by your child's mantra of, "Me! Me! Me! Want! Want! Want! Now! Now! Now!" try to focus beyond this.

Remember that it's temporary and survivable and keep in mind the loving and adorable moments of connection. These are lasting and will help shield both you and your child from whatever the world may throw at you.

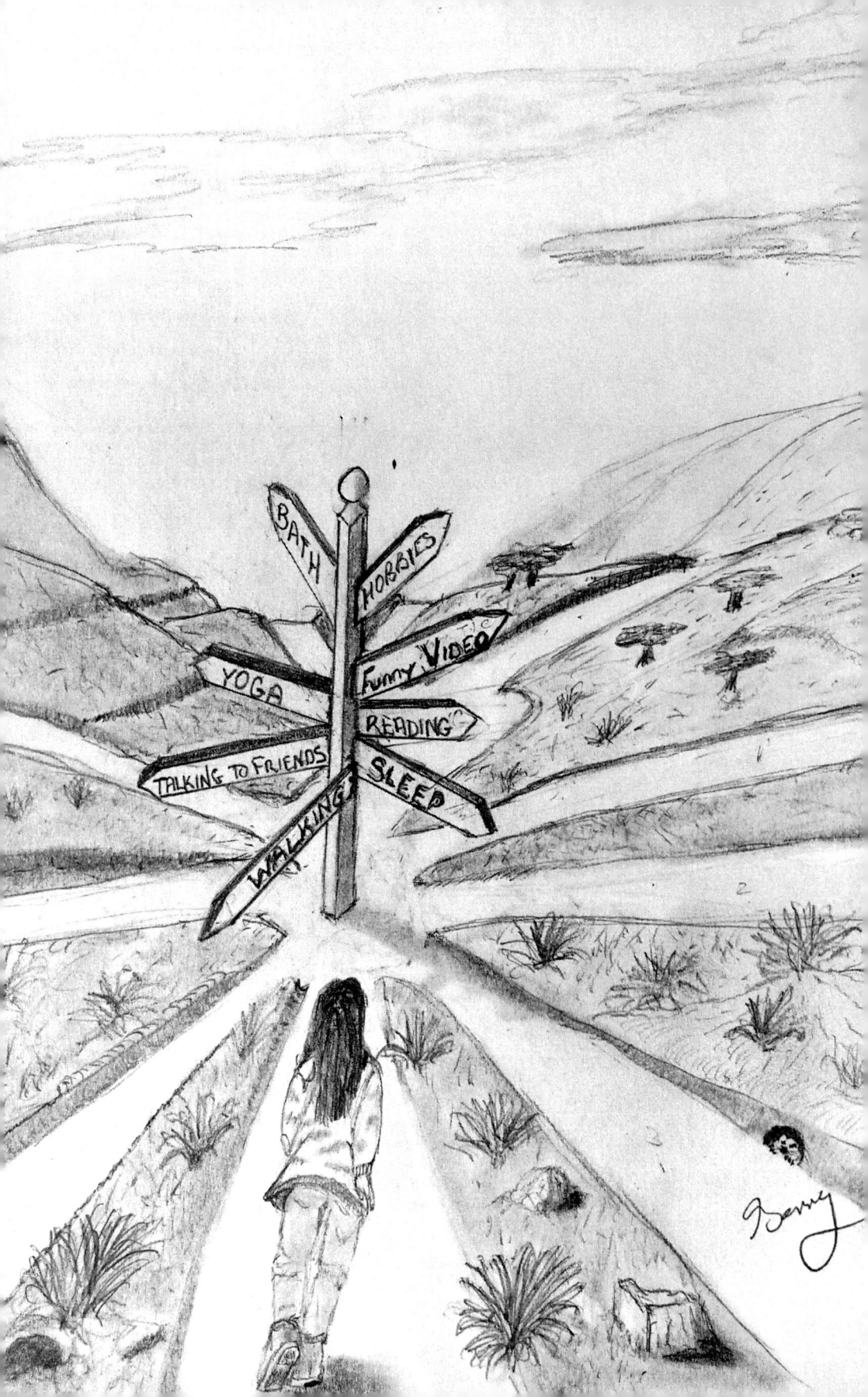

Chapter Three
Importance of Self-Care as a Parent

I vividly recall being snapped back to focus during an enjoyable daydream whilst attending some mandatory conference in my early psychologist years. An elderly gentleman in jeans and a t-shirt took the platform amongst all the suits and ties. He was an American Indian Shaman Chief and his words resonated strongly with what I'd observed in my work.

He said that, "Every child needs at least one adult who believes that they are exceptional and that they are the most important thing in that adult's universe."

Simple but profound. The Shaman's comment echoed aspects of Winnicott's (Paediatrician, Psychoanalyst) notion of 'good enough' parenting.

The question is, how do you do this amongst the seemingly insane demands of a child?

How do you survive your brain imploding when it's being battered to death by the relentless banshee screaming and tortuous chants of "Play with me, look at me, play with me, look at me!"

In order to create a 'good enough' holding environment, it is essential that parents take care of themselves so that they feel 'held' and have the emotional space to cope with the child's needs. Hopefully, it is possible to take a break to go for a walk, spend an hour in a coffee shop, read, go to a yoga class, or whatever other way you choose to create a 'protected space' where you can replenish your energy. If you don't have the support of family or friends, there are community services that can help. Please don't feel guilty about reaching out to them. It will not harm your child to be minded by a caring, responsible adult for an hour on occasion.

Children learn to self soothe when tired or distressed by observing how their parents soothe themselves. By taking care of yourself, you are also modelling helpful coping mechanisms to your child.

It can often help to write a list of thoughts and activities that give you pleasure. These moments get quickly shadowed and swallowed by the busyness and demands of being a parent, partner, working and keeping the household from falling into chaos! Writing these thoughts down can be a way of binding them into memory and action. An opening for these self-care activities rarely spontaneously presents itself. It almost always requires a strong commitment to equate the need for 'self' time with other essential human needs such as sleep, food and water. 'Self' time is not the same as being 'selfish' as this 'self' time is essential for sufficient emotional health to be able to 'give' to others. It results in emotional healing and nourishment.

It is common that as you witness and experience your child's world, it brings to mind memories of your own childhood. Intense emotions related to unresolved childhood traumatic incidents may emerge and lead to anxiety and depression. This may be resolved by working through the grief using the therapeutic part of the world (e.g. family, friends, nature, hobbies). However, if intense emotions feel 'stuck' it may require a period of therapy to help to work through these issues. Whichever path is required, by resolving these issues you're giving yourself and your child a gift. It frees you to be more yourself and more able to be thoughtful and present in your child's world.

By shedding old cloaks of self-criticism and doubt and giving yourself permission to have 'breathing space', you can fully become involved and enjoy the playful moments.

Travelling side by side on your child's journey through life can be an amazing, exhilarating and fun-filled experience (despite a few hellish spots).

To enter the world of a child is to see through the anticipation and eyes of the famous bear, Winnie the Pooh, who stated, "As soon as I saw you, I knew an adventure was going to happen."

Taking care of yourself leaves you open to notice, enjoy and treasure the adventures with your child.

Chapter Four
How Parental Relationship Affects the Child

We all have memories of tension between our parents. I clearly recall my father frustrating my mother such that I thought her eyeballs would roll out of her head, fall in the dog bowl and forever disappear in the inner world of a Labrador! Similarly, memories of my father muttering guttural sounds under his breath when my mother crashed the car by driving through a box (being adamant that the stationary, inanimate object was at fault) also come to mind.

The odd spark of conflict is inevitable but when it becomes common behaviour rather than a rarity it is problematic.

The relationship of the family provides the child with a separate link to each parent and a link between the parents that exclude the child. If this can be tolerated, it provides a prototype for a relationship in the role of witness rather than participant. This gives the capacity for seeing ourselves in relation to others, for considering a different point of view while still retaining our own and for being able to observe and relate to others while still being ourselves.

A strong relationship between parents provides the infant with "a rock to which he can cling and against which he can kick" (Winnicott, 1964).

If the parental couple is missing in the mother's or father's mind, it can cause difficulties in the infant's ability to think clearly and creatively (Feldman, 1989). It can lead to impaired cognitive and social development and increases children's anxiety. The nature of the parental relationship also affects how children perceive both 'masculine' and 'feminine' identity. Marital disharmony undermines the quality of parenting.

The nature of children is that they are egocentric, so they feel responsible for their parent's dissonance with the accompanying guilt. Sometimes, parents caught up in their own emotional minefields, encourage children to take sides in parental disputes. Some parents, inadvertently, stress children by feeling "bad" about themselves and/or in their relationship. Parents can subconsciously turn to their children to meet their emotional needs.

Fathers often hit barriers to being more involved with their children due to employers, media and even the mother who may feel threatened about the father being more involved with the child. It's important to be respectful of your partner's different style of parenting. Different is not necessarily wrong! Mothers actually have great power to actively encourage and support fathers. The shift in power and status which inevitably occurs after childbirth for both parents and the emotional resurgence of past traumas from a parent's childhood can trigger discord and resentment.

A parent's happiness leads to a nurturing parental holding environment which gives children a sense of safety and predictability. It models a way of intimacy, dispute resolution, emotional expression and respect and it becomes the basis for the child's future relationships.

Research shows that two thirds of couples experience a drastic drop in the quality of their relationship within three years of the birth of a child. It is crucial to create an armoury to protect the sanctity of the parental relationship.

IDEAS
- Develop a culture of appreciation – thank each other for the small powerful thoughtful moments (e.g., making dinner, taking the bins out).
- Use "I" statements and try to avoid criticism. If a contentious topic needs to be raised – begin the conversation with praise and acknowledgement of the great things your partner does.
- Small rituals of connection – e.g., go for walks together (even if baby is travelling with you in the pram), eat dinner together without the TV and talk together (not just about the kids), play together (e.g., see a movie, play a board game), kiss when you leave each other and reunite, hug before going to sleep each night, text random caring thoughts (e.g., looking forward to you coming home).
- Laugh together at least 10-15 minutes per day!
- Seek professional help if needed.

Chapter Five
Beyond Daddy Baby Blue's

The dream. Pure joy. Baby Bliss. Happy Happy. You see yourself as the Dad in 'The Incredibles'.

The Reality. Sleepless nights. Banshee screaming (infant and mother). Fights with your partner. Struggling with work and exhaustion. Nothing's funny. Not much to look forward to; anxious, trouble sleeping, miserable, irritable, angry, withdrawing, feeling powerless, hopeless.

This continues over weeks and feels endless. The realisation that 'The Incredibles' is a fictional cartoon sinks in.

These are all signs of Paternal Post Natal Depression (PPND).

One in ten fathers suffer from PPND. Stress is highest in the first year and seems to occur or intensify when the baby is three months old. Usually with the birth of a baby, the family has to survive on one income. Often the mother cares for the infant which puts a lot of pressure on the father to financially support the family, be a good dad and a good partner.

Roles and responsibilities in the family are redefined with the arrival of a baby, not just amongst siblings but also amongst the parents. Dads often feel abandoned by their partner who's absorbed by caring for the infant.

PPND is different from the 'daddy blues' that many fathers experience which can be relieved with extra sleep, exercise and being with friends. With PPND these strategies

barely scratch the surface. It is different to what women experience in that it often appears later after the birth and develops over the course of the first year. PPND can be hard to spot, as depression in men can look very different to what's expected. Rather than appearing sad, men often hide this as they perceive it as a sign of being weak and vulnerable at a time when they feel it is expected that they be strong and protective of the family. Society, especially for men, has an attitude that sad feelings should be just 'sucked up' and not expressed. Obviously, the flaw in this notion is that people are humans, not vacuum cleaners. Mind even vacuum cleaners need to be emptied at times otherwise they fail and possibly explode.

People need to appropriately express intense emotions to retain mental health. The sadness could take on the form of anger and irritability. The person may work constantly, become impulsive and/or get lost in obsessive behaviours (e.g., drinking, gambling, shopping sprees, over-eating, affairs).

Sadness, loss of pleasure in activities, feelings of worthlessness, powerlessness and suicidal thoughts can also occur. Memory and ability to organise can become affected and they may suffer physical symptoms like headaches, tiredness and muscular aches.

If mothers observe significant changes in their partner's behaviour and start to wonder "who the hell is he!", it's worth a trip to the GP to help work out what's going on. Dads often go undiagnosed as they are less willing to ask for help and are often inadvertently excluded from situations when their symptoms may be assessed. Although mothers have regular follow-up visits with doctors after the baby's birth either for themselves or for the baby's health, dads are usually busy working during these appointments and don't attend.

As a result, they are not asked the useful questions by their doctor which may reveal suffering and result in treatment.

Men go through hormone changes after the birth of the baby as testosterone decreases and other hormones such as oestrogen increases. These hormone changes, combined with sleep deprivation which also affects hormones, can in itself create a 'storm' of epic proportions. Some dads feel incompetent, overwhelmed, worthless and alone. Whatever the feeling, the reality is that dads are very precious to their baby.

The first step to getting help would be to talk to your doctor who could give you some strategies and can also refer you to an appropriate psychologist/counsellor. Sometimes medication can help but it's not always necessary. Counselling sessions can give you more strategies to help cope and also provide a safe space to talk through feelings.

Without treatment PPND leads to more nightmares. Not just for Dad but for all the family.

Relationships end in divorce, jobs are lost causing more financial stress, physical health problems develop, and destructive behaviours take their toll.

Truth. Depression and anxiety are just as common and real as physical problems like heart disease and diabetes. They can also be as soul and life threatening. Facing up to being depressed is not a defeat. It's taking control of your life and admitting that there's hope.

Like Mr Incredible you can rescue your world from destruction. Just remember that even Mr Incredible couldn't do it on his own and needed help.

RISK FACTORS OF PPND
- Fifty percent of men whose partners suffer from Post Natal Depression will become depressed themselves.
- A lack of support from friends and family.
- Financial stress
- Relationship difficulties with their partner before birth of the baby.
- History of depression, anxiety or other mood disorders.
- Being a perfectionist.
- Having had a difficult relationship with own father.
- A sick baby or a baby who is having trouble sleeping.
- Sleep deprivation.

RESOURCES
Beyond Blue-information about depression
Just Speak Up-government website about Post Natal Depression
postpartumdads.org
The Shed Online-community online discussion group for men
saddaddy.com
PANDA (Post and Antenatal Depression Association)
Lifeline 13 11 14 (telephone counselling available 24hours/day)

Chapter Six
The Magic of Fathers

A friend recounted the tale of his father re-tiling the bathroom and gluing the tiles upside down – thus creating the effect of the inverted bamboo jungle. The family aware of the unintentional surreal aspect, embraced this quirk and it became a fond memory. Perhaps this is the essence of the power of fathers. The love they can forge with their children is so strong that it defies criticism and encourages playfulness.

Take a moment to recall positive moments with your father. Your mind may be full of great memories or it may be hard, or even impossible to find. Even if not found with your father, it may be found with another fathering figure (uncle, teacher, kind stranger etc).

All these memories (even bad ones which can strengthen your resolve to do different and better) are bits of magic that you can use to be a 'good enough' father.

Research has shown that fathering has a significant impact on social, cognitive, emotional and physical wellbeing throughout the child's life. Children need time with fathers and father-like figures and it plays a major part in protecting children from the emotional stresses of life. An American report in 2000 found that children without appropriate fathering are four times more likely to have emotional and behavioural problems than children with appropriate fathering.

Winnicott observed that good enough parenting could be

done by both mother and father. There are both female and male psychic elements in every human. Thus, fathers all have potential to be nurturing, thoughtful and caring and to not just be restricted to the practical, protective, financial-provider role.

The father's role with the new-born is protecting the mother-child dyad by providing a secure environment for the mother. This is achieved by offering physical and emotional support. Hormonal studies have shown that fathers have increased levels of oxytocin during the first weeks of their baby's life. Known as the 'love hormone', it increases feelings of bonding amongst groups. This hormone is elevated when fathers play with the baby (Journal Biological Psychiatry, 2010). Thus, dads get a 'love buzz' which rewards and encourages more playing interaction with the baby. The 'macho' hormone, testosterone (associated with aggressive behaviour) also declines in fatherhood (Journal Proceedings of the National Academy of Sciences) possibly reducing the urge to risk-take and encouraging nurturing.

Fathers also have a role in playing with babies and in holding in mind their love, pride, warmth and hope towards the infant. Psychoanalytic literature speaks of the mother acting as a mirror to the child, her facial expression of feelings reflecting back to the child that they are unique, lovable and the most important person in the mother's life. I believe that this phenomenon also exists in the father's gaze upon their child. The father is usually the first person to come into the child's life from outside the mother-baby dyad. There is thought, that the mother and father occupy two different, but not exclusive, mental domains in the

child. The mother's domain is more that of nurturing, comforting and attending to needs, whereas the father's domain is more boundary-setting and reality testing which encourages the infant to tolerate frustration and become resilient. Father's play seems to encourage more muscular activity, exploration of body and space. Fathers offer an alternative attachment figure and a bridge to the external world. The father assists the infant in separation from the mother in spending time alone with the infant. He is the model that represents progression, independence and activity. Numerous studies indicate that an active, nurturing, thoughtful style of fathering is associated with better verbal skills, intellectual functioning and academic achievement. An appropriate adult male model helps boys develop positive gender role characteristics and helps girls to form positive opinions of men and to relate to them. Fathers often struggle to know how to provide appropriate fathering and although every child-father relationship is unique, there are some tips on how to create 'good enough' fathering.

These can be drawn from your own positive memories of being fathered as a child, from your observations of how fathers act in the world and from your own inspiration.

One of my clients, came home early from work on a cold wet day and on impulse bought his six-year-old son some hot chocolate during his lunch time at school. Another father gave his young daughter strawberry ice cream and an origami Swan when she was sick with a bad cold. These thoughtful, unexpected acts cement the connection between father and child.

These acts are the breath that brings to life the feelings of love for your child. I often see families, where, although it is clear that the parents do love their child, the child does not feel or believe that their parents love them. In some of these situations, it is likely that words of affection are not followed through with enough thought and action.

- Be proactive and thoughtful. Create cherished memories and fathering rituals.
- It is important to have unique shared activities and time alone with each child in the family. For example, if you and your older son enjoy 'footy' but your younger son does not, it is important to find an activity or interest that both you and your younger son mutually enjoy. Similarly, it is important that fathers find a common unique interest with each of their daughters.
- It is crucial to be physically and mentally present. As much as possible interrupt what you are doing to listen to your child. Try to turn off work when you are home and make the focus of your attention on your partner and children the priority.
- Create family rituals to celebrate positive events(e.g., school reports, kindness/generosity) and rites of passage (e.g., beginning kindergarten, learning to ride a bike).
- Use car travel to listen and talk with your child. Amazing conversations can happen during school and sport drop off and pick up.
- Email and write to your children if you are away from home for long periods.

Phone calls are great but often young children find it

hard to talk and focus on a phone call. An email or note is something tangible which they can hold onto and look over at any time.

• Randomly leave notes and 'treasures' for your children to show you think of them.
• Try and have meals with the family.
• Keep promises.
• Laugh and play with your children as much as possible!

At times you may feel useless, redundant and incompetent. Not true! It is true that there is a lot to learn with children. This applies to mothers and fathers alike. It sends you upside down and backwards into a challenging, bizarre but incredibly rewarding world.

The goals to achieve 'good enough' fathering is to aim to always be there when needed, give indestructible, unconditional love and make the child realise that they are unique, special and that you believe that they have the potential to do wonderful things in the world!

The reward is hearing and feeling your child say with their eyes and words "I love you, daddy."

"There are three stages in a man's life; he believes in Santa Claus, he doesn't believe in Santa Claus, he is Santa Claus." – Unknown Author.

The latter stage is that of fathering.

Chapter Seven
Bedraggled Teddy Bears, Blankie and Other Loved Things.

It is not uncommon to observe some odd behaviour in parents of young children such as rummaging hysterically in garbage bins in the middle of the night, wildly chasing after buses and taxis and frantically searching playgrounds and shopping centres. They are desperately searching for a lost teddy bear, stuffed rabbit, bit of blanket, pillow or other precious object which has somehow become attached to their child's soul. To the child, failure to retrieve this special object can feel like the centre of their world has gone!

Often the object has been so exuberantly loved and played with that it's hard to imagine it once resembled a teddy bear, rabbit or doll! This is a normal part of childhood. The loved object is what is known as the 'transitional object'. It develops from the new-born infant's fist-in-mouth activities but is much more than just oral satisfaction.

Infants often adopt an object which gives them comfort when they are separated from their mother. This object becomes an extension of the mother in the child's psyche. It will usually have a similar feel and scent to the mother and reminds them of warmth and protectiveness. Winnicott (Paediatrician, Psychoanalyst) called this the 'transitional object' in that it helps the infant to make the transition from the 'me' to the 'not me'. This occurs at around four to six months when the child is moving towards the external world but is not yet separated from the internal world. It allows the child to let go of the mother and develop independence. It is the first creative act, as a child creates reality out of their imagination.

For example, a teddy bear (transitional object) joins the family for dinner each night. The bedraggled bear at the table with its empty bowl of invisible bear food is a reality, but it has been borne out of the child's imagination. Playing with the transitional object occurs in the 'potential' space which is at the intersection of the self and other and is the beginning of individuation. It is also in this space that play occurs.

There are several special qualities in the child's relationship with the transitional object. The object must survive instinctual loving and hating (even mutilation and pure aggression). The child has a feeling of omnipotence over the object and it must never change unless changed by the child. Its fate is not to be forgotten or mourned but to lose meaning as the child matures. At this time, the transitional phenomena have been diffused to the whole 'playing' space shared in relationships.

Ideally, the mother lets the object get dirty and even smelly, as washing it can cause a break in the continuity of the infant's experience and destroy the meaning and value. Of course, there are times when it must be cleaned as a matter of hygiene. This requires stealth! It is helpful to have a spare 'transitional object' which can be rotated when the child is distracted. Rotation is important, otherwise the spare won't have the special scent which makes it seem like the original. If a spare isn't possible – working out

an acceptable substitute may help. If the object has to be cleaned, hand wash it as much as possible. As the child gets older, they could be encouraged to help bath their special bear or blanket.

So, when your child drags around a mutilated, dirty, smelly, dilapidated precious object; looks into whatever is left of its eyes, whispers into its ear and demands that it too have a cookie – please keep in mind its meaning. It is a bridge, not only connecting the child to you, but eventually connecting the child to the outer world.

Chapter Eight
Imaginary Friends

As a result of a soul piercing scream as I reversed down the driveway, I discovered my daughter's imaginary friends in the shape of a tribe of invisible Meerkats. According to my daughter, they were different colours but their 'leader' was the yellow one. Apparently, he was clinging to the underside of the car, scared and shocked but otherwise unscathed. We would often take them to see their 'cousins' at the zoo. My daughter was fascinated with rainbows and she collectively named the Meerkats the 'ROYGBVs' which was an acronym for the six colours of the rainbow. The ROYGBVs sometimes joined us at the dinner table… all six of them…quite a crowd! Luckily, these Meerkats had reasonable table manners.

No, my daughter and I are not having a psychotic episode. This is the domain of imaginary friends. They come as humans, animals, trucks, some in herds, anything is possible in this world. About 65% of children develop imaginary friends between the ages of three to five years. This is a time when they start to form their own identities and test the boundaries between phantasy and reality. Nearly half continue to play with imaginary friends through to age seven.

It is important to be respectful of your child's need for an imaginary friend. No one, including siblings, should ridicule, tease or belittle the child. Imaginary friends are true to these children and this is very different to lying.

The imaginary friend needs to come from the child's imagination not the parent's imagination. If the imaginary friend's behaviour is altered by the parent's imagination, this becomes manipulation, not playing. Children vividly experience interactions with their imaginary friends but they know that these friends are not real. Maybe imaginary friends represent 'bemagination' – something in between belief and imagination. Oldest children, only children and those who don't watch much TV are more likely to create an imaginary friend. This likely reflects opportunity as unstructured time alone is required to construct an imaginary friend.

Imaginary friends enable children to try out different relationships at a critical point in their social development. A child scolding an imaginary friend is an imaginative way of trying to understand concepts of authority. Children blaming their imaginary friend for 'knocking over the milk' is a perfectly 'normal' strategy for a child to deal with their guilt. Imaginary friends help children to test out their feelings and actions. They allow the child to be in control and in charge at a time in their life when very little is in their control. They permit them to have a private life without adult presence and assists them to deal with intense emotions. Imaginary friends are part of normal development.

Parents can use imaginary friends to gain valuable insights into how a child is coping and take action. Anxiety associated with major changes in a child's life such as a new baby or divorce can be reflected in play with their imaginary friend. For example, if your child was spending

a lot more time than usual with their imaginary friend just before moving to a new house, it may indicate that they were sad or anxious about the move even if they had not verbalised their distress.

There are situations when an imaginary friend, along with other factors, can indicate a problem. If a child has no friends and no interest in forming friendships, engages in violent and hurtful behaviour, appears fearful of the imaginary friend or complains that the imaginary friend won't go away, there is reason for concern.

Research shows that children with imaginary friends tend to be creative, focussed with good attention span, self-directed in play and grasp the difference between 'real and pretend' (exception being magical beings like Santa Claus, Tooth Fairy and the Easter Bunny as our culture actively encourages the suspension of disbelief of these creatures). They are emotionally well adjusted, intellectually and verbally skilled, outgoing and advanced in understanding social relationships.

Stephen Hawkings stated that "imaginary time is a new dimension, at right angles to ordinary, real time". Some believe that this dimension is where playing and imaginary friends live.

Chapter Nine
Meaning of Childhood Games

As children grow, they go through different developmental stages, but there are several things which remain consistent, one of which is the incessant chant of "Play with me, play with me, play with me!" whether delivered by words or by the hopeful look in a child's eyes.

Simple children's games can be extremely powerful in a child's development. For example, the common game of 'Hide and Seek' involves important attachment processes such as object permanence (objects still exist even though they can't be seen, touched or heard), secure attachment (I can find you if I need to and you can find me if I hide), object constancy (a relationship can continue despite separations and reunions) and trust (worthiness of self and reliability of others). Games developing object permanence and connection are commonly observed such as the use of toy telephones and toilet rolls connected by string to make 'walkie-talkies'.

Cuddling a soft toy animal or doll helps a child learn how to rely on their own ability to seek comfort and to nurture. It encourages children to try out phrases, tones of voice and expression and to safely act out scenarios.

Vigorous play helps diffuse excess physical and emotional energy and stimulate 'happy' chemicals (endorphins) in the body. The ancient game of 'chasings' in all its various forms (Tag, Tip, Bullrush etc.), allows children to explore different roles such as pursuer/pursued and hero/villain.

Games of contest and trials of strength like 'King/Queen of the Mountain' is a wonderful expression of rivalry.

Games such as 'I spy' and 'Who am I' develops skills by testing powers of observation and promotes a sense of mastery. Sorting the world into categories helps children to understand and connect with their environment. Various studies have given evidence that language greatly influences visual attention. If a child is shown a picture of what they need to find, it takes longer than if they are verbally told what to search for. This suggests that language improves working memory. Children learn in the real world and this is a very 'cluttered' place! If a child doesn't know where to look – it becomes hard to learn. Thus, games that encourage learning language are developmentally very important.

Constructive play such as building blocks (e.g., Lego, Meccano), craft (creating cities from discarded cardboard boxes, collages, paper mache etc) can be extremely helpful in softening a stressful situation in a child's life. Common stressors for children can be starting school, moving to a new home, home renovations, being sick or their parent being sick or having relatives move in for a long period of time.

'Doing and undoing' is common in many games such as building towers and then knocking them down. It develops the concept that out of destruction, creation can arise and raises hopefulness and perseverance.

'Make-believe' games allow the child to explore different ways of being in the world. Pretend games involving roles like fireman, doctor, police and vet allow the child to take on protector/rescuer role which helps them feel some control over their world and gives a sense of mastery. These games allow the expression of both positive and negative feelings, the modulation of affect and ability to integrate emotion with cognition. They are the forerunners to developing the capacity for self-regulation including reduced aggression, delay of gratification and development of social skills and empathy.

These are just a few examples of how play develops skills, connection, identity and competence.

So please, hold this in mind, as you strangely morph into a vigorous, sprinting meerkat joining the pouncing leopard with superpowers (alias your child) in taming a wild mysterious jungle (alias the lounge room) that 'games' have incredible meaning and worth.

Chapter Ten
The Importance of Playing in Building Resilience

Donald Winnicott (Paediatrician, Psychoanalyst) observed the importance of play in children. Play is spontaneous given a 'good enough' environment where the child feels; thought of, held, understood and loved. It is important in the mastery of anxiety and communication. Play has become so acknowledged that it is recognised by the United Nations High Commission as the right of every child. Playing opens up a space such that a creative 'reaching out' can take place, which in turn leads to connection and resilience.

In the 'playing space' a child becomes totally absorbed in the emotions and content of the play. Parents often observe a child playing who becomes so fused with the play, that it seems that even if a stampede of purple rabid elephants rampaged through the house, they would be oblivious and just continue playing. It is a similar phenomenon to what we experience in adult playing, when we become engrossed in a book, movie or music and lose track of time.

Unstructured free play gives children opportunity to discover their own interests and competencies and protects them from excessive stress. Sadly, there is a great deal of pressure on parents to expose their children to a pandemonium of structured activities. Parents often feel that they are failing their child if they are not involved in dance, soccer, rugby, singing, art classes, gymnastics, languages, trapeze skills, lion taming etc! Children (and their exhausted parents) are often bolting from one structured activity after the other with little opportunity for unstructured play. The key is finding a balance amongst education, structured play, unstructured play, eating and sleep.

When play is 'child-driven', children explore and create worlds which they can master which leads to increased confidence and resilience. Undirected play with other children allows them to learn to share, negotiate and advocate for themselves. Vigorous play helps diffuse excess physical and emotional energy and stimulate 'happy' chemicals (endorphins) in the body.

Parents have the opportunity to connect with their children through unstructured play. By letting the child direct the play, the parent gains unique insight into the way the child feels and how they see their universe and it can form a bridge connecting the inner worlds of child and parent. The child has the parent's full attention (no phones, computers, housework etc) and feels that they are heard, respected and are the most important person in their parent's life. This develops their self-worth.

Facilitating play with other children is enormously helpful in assisting your child's ability to interact with their peers. Especially, for a school-age child, a one-to-one play situation with another child gives opportunity to practise sharing, empathy and co-operation. Under the thoughtful, sensitive gaze of Mum or Dad, a child can be subtly guided and flourish in the often tough world of peer relationships.

Play develops resilience as it gives a child a sense of control in the world and builds connectiveness. So, when

you see your child engrossed in play, and you feel guilty that your child is just playing rather than being occupied with structured learning, focus on the fact that unstructured play is essential for learning and development. Einstein stated that play is the 'highest form of research'. Healthy psychological life is not just the absence of symptoms but a real engagement with playful creation and the seeds of this are in childhood.

Chapter Eleven
The Effect of Violence in Media on Children

My family and I frequently explore local community fairs and I'm often struck by the number of children running around excitedly with toy weapons of mass destruction! The gleeful but eerie sounds 'Bang! Bang! You're dead' in tune with the sound of a toy bazooka or HK417 machine gun are somewhat disturbing. It's true that toy guns have been around since children could hold a stick, but it's the realism of these toys that is really horrifying. In truth, it's pretty scary that a child even knows what an HK417 is!

When horrific violent incidents have occurred and been attributed to media influence, on deeper examination, media has been just one of many other factors building up and influencing the person's behaviour.

Research has strongly indicated that reducing violent behaviour in society requires much more than just reducing and monitoring images of violence in the media. It requires effective weapon control and commitment and action to deal with issues which drive destructive aggression, such as child abuse, poverty and mental health issues. Albeit, media violence may have still been a contributing factor to the violence.

Throughout history, children have played 'Cowboys and Indians', 'cops and robbers' and other similar games which have an element of violence in them. However, the issues with violence in the media is that it is often very

graphic, fast-moving and appears realistic. This can have a profoundly detrimental effect on children. Children are intrigued by images but don't have the cognitive ability to make connections and they tend to focus on the more intense scenes rather than the story.

Problems are more likely to occur for children who are less able to differentiate between fiction and reality, and for those less cognitively able to deal with their emotions and with aggressive images and ideas. This is related to age, cognitive ability, sensitivity and maturity. Research clearly shows that prolonged exposure to media violence is a factor which may lead to children displaying aggressive behaviour. Viewing violence may also lead to desensitisation to real violence, reduction of empathy for others and can induce anxiety that the world is a frightening place.

Parents need to be in control of what their children are exposed to, and it is important to not just rely on the rating of the game or movie. There can be a great deal of difference between two movies rated PG. with the busyness of life, it can be very tempting to use a TV or game console as a 'babysitter'. As long as this is not a regular and lengthy occurrence there is no problem in doing this, but the TV show or game must be carefully selected.

Children should be reminded that media violence is fictional. Unfortunately, there can often be extremely graphic incidents displayed on the news and it is crucial to monitor your child's exposure and response to these scenes. Your child will be influenced by your beliefs, so if you express that violence is not condoned in real life and screen the level of violence in their media viewing, this will have a huge positive impact. An adult helping a child interpret and critique the media material lessens the negative effect. Every child is unique and responds differently to violence in the media. Sadly, the increase in amount and intensity of violence in media is a direct reflection of the increase in frustration, despair and violence in society. It cannot be easily avoided, especially as your child gets older and is more influenced by peers and community, but it can be managed at a pace that matches their developing cognition, maturity and sensitivities.

It is highly recommended to not have a media device (e.g., TV, computer) in a child's bedroom. Children left to watch violent media without responsible adult supervision is a great danger. It is a crucial role of parents to guide their children to develop a thoughtful inner awareness as they watch media which reflects upon their internal moral/ethical code of behaviour.

Discussing, highlighting and role modelling alternate forms of conflict resolution is also very important and provides children with alternate ways of dealing with the world without resorting to violence. Educating children about 'heroic' people who spoke and acted against violence in the world in a non-violent manner, helps to balance out the effects of media violence.

It's unlikely that decreasing and monitoring children's viewing of violent media will result in them chanting Gandhi's words of "An eye for an eye leaves the world blind."

However, it will allow them to enjoy age-appropriate development, which will strengthen their ability to navigate the future of media violence. Surely, children enjoying age-appropriate development should be an unalienable human right!

Chapter Twelve
The Creature That Ate My Child!

In my dream, I relive sitting on the floor with my daughter playing with the little ponies while the little people are having a tea party in Teddy Land. Her warm little body nestled so close, she's almost sitting on top of me. I wake and go to stir my daughter from her sleep to prepare for school. I quietly open her door, raise the blind to let a sliver of light in to gently beckon the morning.

I kiss the soft bundle cocooned in her blanket on the forehead only to be met by a banshee scream of, "I know! I know! I'm up! Get out!"

Yes, my daughter has become a teenager.

Sometime later, I return and knock at the door only to be met with, "Don't come in! I'm getting dressed!"

Either my daughter has an obsession with changing her clothes many times a day or she has adopted this catch cry as a way of stopping her parents interrupting her in her 'cave'. I favour the latter option and in a playful, more open moment she has actually smilingly admitted to her cunning plan.

Adolescence is the time where not only hormones play havoc with your child's emotions and body but so too do the challenges of adapting to many changes in their life. Greater academic and peer pressures, expectations to be more responsible and to live up to expectations of media and society put great stress on teenagers. Many of these expectations (especially highlighted by media) are

unrealistic and inappropriate.

Messages such as 'man up', 'woman up', 'be beautiful', 'be skinny', 'don't be too skinny' and 'be cool' are extremely damaging. The essence of adolescence is immaturity! They are not adults. They are in between a world of child and adult where they often feel that everything is out of their control. Not only has their body become an alien entity of smelliness and hairiness, but they feel that they have little choices in their life. They have to go to school and study what the school determines that they should study, and they have to live by the family's rules and routines.

Whereas childhood focused on appropriate attachment, adolescence is the journey of appropriate detachment. Its goal is a mutual letting go which gives freedom to develop independence and identity. This requires a transformation of both parents and adolescent. Separating from parents (with more dependence on peers), accepting challenges and risks, curiosity, autonomy, maturity, negative attitude (boredom, criticism, complaints), active and passive resistance to authority and testing limits are part of the adolescent's journey. Disorganisation (what used to work with your child doesn't anymore), critical and negative attitude (child's more difficult behaviour causes more criticism), active and passive resistance and irritability (in response to adolescent's active and passive resistance and irritability) and anxiety (triggered by adolescent limit testing) is the parent's journey.

Some adolescents struggle more than others; depending on their family background, personality and life traumas which can put more stress on the family. The parent's crucial role is to remain firm in limits and values while

not being overly punitive. Adolescence is a mixture of negotiation seeking 'middle ground' coupled with certain non-negotiable rules. For example, what your child wears for a casual dinner is negotiable but their curfew is not.

One way of illustrating this negotiation is the 'biscuit and tea (or coffee)' philosophy. Dunking a biscuit successfully into a warm liquid is an art form of negotiation. If the biscuit is dunked too long, it dissolves into a soggy, gritty mess in the bottom of the cup. A bit like the fate of a parent who gives in too often to adolescent demands. However, if it's not dunked long enough it remains hard and relatively bland and doesn't absorb the flavour of the tea. This is symbolic of the parent who is mostly uncompromising and unable to accept and value that their child is developing their own different unique thoughts and desires.

It is in fact, quite a useful philosophy in life to seek the 'middle ground' for both parent and adolescent. Similarly, 'common ground' is another territory worthy of exploration and adoption into the 'new world' of parent and emerging adolescents. Re-developing common interests between yourself and your adolescent even if it largely revolves around a TV series that you both enjoy strengthens your connection with them. It also encourages the healthy notion that 'playing' continues in the adult world albeit it is a different form to playing as a child. Playing with little ponies doesn't really cut it anymore! More adult playing consists of books, sport, movies, music, art, entertaining conversations and more sophisticated games. This 'playing' with your adolescent is still crucial although it also must be balanced with their need for independence and for 'peer time' and 'me time'.

Although having an adolescent in the family can be difficult – it can be hugely rewarding. They can be incredibly exuberant, creative, playful, idealistic and appropriately rebellious with a strong sense of fairness and justice.

My thoughts wander to my 13-year-old daughter who recently barged into the kitchen excitedly announcing that, "Doctors in Melbourne were revolting!"

It took a while to work it out, but she was actually ecstatic that they were defiantly standing up to the Australian Government to help refugee children. I suggested that I thought the word she wanted was 'protesting' not 'revolting'. We both thought this error was extremely funny and laughed. Adolescents can be, in fact, adorable and hilarious!

Chapter Thirteen
My Child Has Been Swallowed by a Teenage Onesie – A Survivor's Guide

So, you have begun your journey with your child into adolescence! Don't despair. Most have more adorable adolescent moments than Terrible Teens moments. Yesterday, I walked into our study to find my 13-year-old daughter and her friend engaged in happy chatter and laughter. The adolescent twist in this scene is that my daughter was lying spread-eagled on her stomach on top of the air hockey table eating chips while chatting to her friend. She was in absolute bliss enjoying the cold air from the table on her body and the connection of friendship. I went back in 10 minutes later and she was still lying on the air hockey table but this time the dog had joined her on the table and she and her friend were teaching our confused canine yoga positions. With my teenage daughter life is full of wild, fascinating and often very funny moments.

It's not always joyful but there are strategies (which do not involve illicit drugs, strong liquor and violence) which can help to survive the more prickly moments.
- 'Common ground' is a territory worthy of exploration in the 'new world' of parent and emerging adolescent. Re-developing common interests strengthens your connection with them. It also encourages the healthy notion that 'playing' continues in the adult world albeit

in a different form.
- 'Pick your battles' is another helpful motto. Decide on the three most important issues that concern you as parents. Bizarre dress and a bedroom that resembles the aftermath of a hurricane may be left for another day or even tolerated, but teenagers not letting you know where they are or when they'll be home is not.
- Be specific in your comments. Rather than saying, "Be more responsible," elaborate by saying, "I feel that it's important that you be more responsible in getting ready for school by making sure your bag is packed and that you get up in time."
- Follow through with what you say. If you stated that if they make one more disrespectful comment their phone will be confiscated, remove the phone after the next disrespectful comment! If you renege (often just from pure exhaustion) your teenager will have no faith that you mean what you say.
- Be empathic by 'putting yourself in their shoes'.
- Criticise behaviour not the person.
- Treat conflict as a form of communication. See your child as an informant not an opponent. If the discussion feels too anger-fuelled, suggest you both have some space and regroup in an hour to discuss more over a glass of water, soft drink or coffee.
- Ask your teenager to educate you about their interests which you know little about. Even if you know that you will never really be interested in cricket or Minecraft, showing a sincere curiosity in what your child finds fascinating about these activities creates a bridge between the two of you.

- Respecting privacy is very important. Many parents are intensely curious about what their teenager is doing for all those hours in their room. Fears of them using drugs, being inappropriate on the internet, evil cult involvement, communicating with aliens or just slothing all day may abound. In reality they are more likely to be listening to music, watching funny YouTube videos and trying out all sorts of different 'looks' in the mirror. Their 'room' is their own 'no judgement' world which they can control and learn more about being themselves. A space to think, express and release emotions and explore different identities. Knock and wait to be invited.

Adolescents are immature by nature. They are on a confusing and difficult path between childhood and adulthood. To find and be true to themselves they have to test, flaunt, provoke, be apathetic, critical, make mistakes and at times be very, very naughty.

As my lovely, cheeky, rebellious daughter says as she contemplates circling her world with a ring of teenage thrills, "Rather a life of oh wells, than a life of what ifs."

Chapter Fourteen
Aardvarks, Cows and Helicopters

The language of adolescents is often coloured with, "Don't touch me!", "Not fair!", "I'll do it in a minute" (space-time distortion abounds here!), "It's not messy to me!" (obviously the small jungle growing out of the week-old sandwich buried under the bed is a science project and not a health hazard!), "What?" and "I don't know."

I find the last one hilarious in conversations with my daughter.

"Did you pack your school bag?"

"I don't know."

"Is your bag packed?"

"I don't know."

"Are you ready for school tomorrow?"

"I don't know."

"Did you see the herd of purple aardvarks riding alpacas stampede through the lounge room?"

"I don't know."

"Do you think the aardvarks and alpacas will eat all the chocolate biscuits?", (she looks up curiously).

"I don't know."

"Would you like a chocolate biscuit?"

(smiles)

"Yes, please!!!"

The following are some more suggestions to lay a foundation which can help survive the 'not so funny', at times, bordering on hellish times living with adolescents.

- Monitor and be involved with the games your teenager plays on electronic devices. It's the best way to connect and understand what they enjoy while at the same time ensuring that it's age-appropriate. I strongly suggest that if parent's give their teenagers mobile phones and allow them on Facebook (computers/iPad) there is the proviso that the parents are given the password and access to their teenager's activities on these devices. I also recommend that none of these devices be in your child's bedroom when they go to sleep. They are detrimental to sleep and it's not just the inane, annoying friends who suddenly text at 3 am with the earth-shattering news that they've lost one of their socks! There is evidence that the blue light disrupts sleep cycles. Even when a phone is on and not in use, it sends outs an intermittent signal which produces radiation. Educate about safe use of these devices.

It is much easier to clearly set out these parameters with your teenager before you give them the phone and access to Facebook.
- Give time and appropriate space for your teenager to talk to you. Listen to them at the time they want to talk. Adolescents are very much about 'seizing the moment' for communication – otherwise the opportunity may be lost.
- Calmly worry. Rather than catastrophizing and seeming negative, talk about alternate plans.

For example: "I'm sure the party will be great, and others won't go dangerous crazy on alcohol but if they do, it's good to have a safety plan. What are your thoughts?"
- Keep appropriate firm limits. Teenagers may criticise

parents for being 'overprotective', but they are secretly relieved the protection and boundaries are there.
- Advocate freedom of respectful speech! Encourage them to be curious and to share their opinions. This helps them develop assertiveness and confidence and gives opportunity for their ideas to be praised and valued.
- Educate about the cost of independence which is accountability. Where appropriate, let them make their decisions and accept the consequences. It's very important that they have successful decisions acknowledged and praised and that they learn from their own mistakes.
- Self disclose some of the mistakes that you made as a teenager. If you notice that some of your teenager's unhelpful behaviour mirrors your own, use yourself as an example to illustrate some helpful strategies.

For example: "I think you're a lot like me, I can be very impatient. Here are some strategies which I use which seem to help me, maybe they could help you."

- Remember to model the behaviour that you want your teenager to demonstrate. Adolescents have a heightened sense of perception regarding adult hypocrisy!
- Befriend your teenager's friends and take time and effort to chat and get to know them. Never criticise their friends. You can draw your child's attention to concerns about their friends in different ways.

For example, "That was strange that Toby didn't turn up to the movie. There's been a few times that he's stood you and your friends up. What do you think? I'd find it very annoying."

One of the most important strategies is to show them your love even when their 'evil alien' persona takes over. Tell

them that you enjoy their company when you're enjoying time with them. Make a point of cooking their favourite food or treating them to a special snack if they seem sad or confused. Leave the door open for communication even if they seem to shut their door in your face. Just keep gently knocking – they'll open it eventually.

A strategy to survive adolescents involves shifting your perception to a different position. Case in point.

Two cows are standing in a field. One says to the other. "What do you think about this mad cow disease?"

"What do I care?" says the other. "I'm a helicopter enjoying the view of the grass."

The second cow could be psychotic, or it could be seeing past being defined as a cow (with the threat of mad cow disease) and enjoying the view from being a helicopter. If you trap yourself in a definition of being a parent of an 'adolescent' (dread! dread!) it breeds a lot of anxiety. However, you could broaden the picture of yourself and your 'adolescent' to recognise that the 'adolescent' is still the child you love and adore (become the helicopter). It is much easier to see through the shadows and enjoy the magic moments of when your child morphs into a caring, thoughtful, creative and often very funny pre-adult.

"Adolescents are not monsters. They are just people trying to learn how to make it among the adults in the world, who are probably not so sure themselves."

Virginia Satir

Chapter Fifteen
Spartacus and Giant Kookaburra

Walking down the stairs towards the car, my gorgeous 13-year-old daughter and I notice an injured possum lying in the front garden. I had heard the Possum Wars last night and they had sounded ferocious. Of course, we weren't going to leave the little fuzzy to perish! I found a box for the trip to the Vet and my daughter used her recess (an apricot) to try and entice it into the charming box. It looked weak and despite some gentle prodding, didn't have strength to raise its body off the ground. It did however have an intense grip on a stick and the other front paw was waving dangerously around trying to look awesome. The dilemma was how to move the possum into the box without hurting it or/and having ourselves wildly lacerated in the process. My amazing daughter had a spark and ran off. She returned with a piece of plastic in the shape of a half cylinder which was perfect for a 'possum stretcher'. We quickly slipped it under its small body and, despite trying to thwart our attempts to put it in the box by clutching onto its beloved stick and waving it all angles, we finally manoeuvred 'Spartacus' (as we named him) into his box.

As we drove to the Vet, I noticed that something was different about the car – like it was missing something. It was then that I realised that my daughter had removed a piece of the car's interior trim to create the 'possum stretcher'! She was so proud of her resourcefulness it was hard to be angry with her. Luckily, I managed to reattach the trim before her

dad got home and so we all survived (including Spartacus). This adventure takes its place amongst our family memories of kind, creative and funny moments.

It illustrates how it's important to not get tied up in the smaller details such as mutilated car interiors, messy rooms, grunts and seemingly endless 'no's' and 'whatevers' and to keep focus on the 'big picture'. Adolescence doesn't last forever. Endure the spikey bits and treasure the adorable creative moments. The battles will decrease, and a less intense, more rational world will follow.

These are some thoughts to help engage with your adolescent.

- Educate about the cost of independence which is accountability. Where appropriate, let them make their decisions and accept the consequences. It's very important that they have successful decisions acknowledged and praised and that they learn from their own mistakes.
- When setting limits avoid ultimatums and be clear and concise. Make rules achievable and be prepared to explain your decisions. It can help to put rules in writing.
- We all make mistakes and are capable of hurting others. Saying 'sorry' shows that you're brave enough to take responsibility for your actions and that you want to mend the relationship. This applies to both parents and adolescents.

In the five-minute car drive to school, my beguiling teenager spoke about the beautiful kookaburra she saw earlier in the morning. Then with a playful spark in her eye she went on to elaborate how huge it was, in fact, possibly seven foot! I added that I thought I saw its cousin, the six-foot kookaburra. She bounced back saying that she knew

it well and that its name is Shorty. Logically, the seven-foot kookaburra was called Tiny. We continued to fantasise about Shorty and Tiny being recruited by ASIO as spies, possibly dropping encrypted messages in their poo. It was funny, invigorating and a most excellent way to start the day for both of us!

Whenever possible try to focus and highlight the amusing, fun and inspiring moments with your child. Notice them, play with them and remember them.

The brilliance and power of adolescent creativity continually astounds.

Chapter Sixteen
Computer Games – Good or Evil? Or Just a Purple Three-Headed Alpaca?

To many parents, the issue of computer games is like the purple three-headed alpaca in the room. We sometimes pretend it doesn't exist, but all know it's there, it's mysterious, weird and possibly dangerous!

Like it or not, the digital computer age has risen, and community computer games are often an integral part of children's culture. Computer and video games have come under a great deal of attack as being harmful to children's development causing social isolation, obesity, depression, violent behaviour and poor school academic performance. There is evidence that violent computer games can encourage violent behaviour in children. However, much like television, this is partly dependent on the amount of time spent on this activity, the content of the game and the nature of the child. It is essential to set time limits on computer game playing. The American Academy of Paediatrics recommends that children be limited to two hours of total media time a day and that there be no media in children's bedrooms. As long as you thoughtfully supervise your child, computer games are unlikely to become a problem unless there are other troubling issues such as having difficulties making friends and feeling isolated. Dependence on computer games and aggressive behaviour is a symptom of a larger issue.

The reality is that the 'purple three-headed alpaca' is here to stay and so the best strategy is to befriend and tame it.

The most effective way to monitor the computer games that your child plays is to play it with them. Talk to your child about the game that they're playing, and the characters and themes contained in it. Look for games that have strong characters with heroic qualities and strengths that allow children to play cooperatively. Ratings on games are really only a guide and there can be huge variation between two games that have the same rating. The decision should rest with your judgement of the game. It is crucial that parents monitor the age-appropriateness of the game and the nature of the violence depicted. The Australian Classification Board and the Entertainment Software Rating Board has a guide on ratings and on how to set parental controls for the 360, Nintendo Wii and PlayStation 3.

The graphics and option to playing online with other players, for some children, can become intoxicating and addictive. Online games have the added risk that they may encounter other players who may behave inappropriately such as by seeking further contact and/or acting in a suggestive or offensive manner. Generally, a child younger than 12 years old should not play online multiplayer games unless the game is highly secure and has moderated and filtered chat (e.g., Club Penguin). Even then, it is recommended that parents remain aware and guide their children. Children need to be instructed on how to behave online and how to be protected from others abusive behaviour. This is where, ultimately, parents have a role in determining what is suitable for their child.

There is evidence that computer games change the brain's physical structure in a similar way to reading, playing piano or deciphering a map. The combination of concentration and dopamine surges strengthen neural circuits. Computer games can greatly enhance skills such as problem solving, creativity, following instructions (e.g., Angry Birds, Cut the Rope), hand eye coordination, spatial and fine motor skills. Strangely some researchers have indicated that, it is the violent action strategy games which had the strongest beneficial effect on the brain. Many of these more appropriate violent strategy games involve themes of good versus evil and have 'morals' which are pro-society. Games such as SIM City and Age of Empires develop planning, resource management and logistics. Many strategy action games involve multi-tasking, simultaneous tracking, fast analysis and decisions. Online multiplayer games develop teamwork skills. The very popular game of Minecraft is like a 'digital Lego' which involves strategic reasoning and decision-making skills as the player must turn raw materials into tools to defeat monsters in the game. Computer games can also develop computer technical skills, maths and reading skills. The key is limiting the amount of time spent on computer games and monitoring the appropriateness of the content of the game. In other words, the 'purple three-headed alpaca' just needs collar and a leash, obedience training and to be understood to become a safe and stimulating playmate.

Chapter Seventeen
Labels

On a recent family holiday, my darling youngest daughter decided to give us all nicknames (a type of label). She called her older sister 'dead mushroom' as she likes to keep herself in a vague dark sleepy cave (yes, she's a teenager). Her Dad was 'schnapps' largely because she likes saying the word 'schnapps' and because he likes apple schnapps. I was 'schmiggles' also because she likes saying the word. I called her 'asparagus' just because she's quirky and cute (and it made my other daughter feel better about being labelled a 'mushroom').

At times labels are important. They help us to play, organise and think about our world. Labels can help us to understand and discuss a pattern of symptoms and behaviours. This can lead to effective treatment and medication. However, often we are too quick to simplify a complicated situation with labels. We are desperate for a 'quick' solution because we feel overwhelmed and exhausted by the situation. The danger of tying up children with labels, apart from missing the true meaning behind the behaviour, is only seeing the child in the light of that label. Children are extremely complex and there is much more to any child than just 'ADHD' or 'Anxiety Disorder'. In the loudness and struggle of intense symptoms it can be easy to lose sight of this.

As parents we have a huge role in influencing how children write their own stories. If we only see our child's anxiety or dyslexia, that's what they will focus on in themselves. Similarly, if we focus on seeing our child as

'bad', 'stupid', 'selfish', 'just like horrible cousin Fifi' or 'difficult', that is how they will mostly see themselves. Parents are like a mirror to their children. What you reflect back becomes another layer of skin which they wear.

Although this power can be scary, it also means that it can be used to guide your child to author their story in a more helpful way. If you acknowledge and highlight their strengths and the aspects you love about them, this will also be etched inside them. Some aspects of various disorders can be used to do astounding wonders in the world. For example, when the energy of a child with ADHD is harnessed so it does not create dysfunction, they can achieve great acts. In fact, Albert Einstein, Galileo, Mozart and Stephen Hawkings had ADHD. In similar thought, Sir Isaac Newton, Sigmond Freud and WB Yeats had anxiety disorders, Alfred Hitchcock and Charles Darwin had Asperger's Disorder and Thomas Edison and Leonardo da Vinci had dyslexia.

Parents by repetitively echoing messages to their child that reflects their strengths and positive aspects create an armour, which can be used to deflect hurtful labelling throughout their life. You can't always control the school or peer environment, but you can strengthen your child's resilience.

One way of doing this is to highlight this spark of wisdom.

"The heart of the truth is seeing, foremost, a human being. The rest gives information and colour, but stereotypes and labels should never be used to define someone. This diminishes us all. Hold true to yourself regardless of other voices." – Author Unknown

Chapter Eighteen
Perfectionism in Children

I believe seeking perfection is like looking in a dark room with sooty tinted sunglasses searching for a black cat that doesn't exist – it's impossible and therefore full of frustration and angst! I recall many agonising moments with my daughter melting down into full lava-flow eruptions because her ponytail was not 'perfect' as it had (to my eyes, imaginary or invisible) 'bumps'. Similarly, I've experienced broken pencils flying through the air like demented projectiles as they obviously refused to create 'perfect' drawings.

Some children are intense and demanding perfection from birth and have an intrinsic perfectionism, whereas for others it's a learned behaviour influenced by critical parents or teachers who often inadvertently imply that they are not satisfied with a child's performance.

For example, the adult who responds to a child getting 90% in a test by saying, "What happened to the other 10%?" even if it's said as a 'joke', is giving the child the message that 90% isn't good enough.

It is crucial that a child learns to separate their self-worth from their products. Perfectionism disrupts children's natural curiosity to learn and explore. They avoid trying new things for fear of making mistakes, procrastinate, focus on mistakes rather than their achievements, set unrealistic goals, become rigid and obsessive in their thinking and harshly judge themselves. This can lead to anxiety and depression.

As a parent, you may feel helpless to contain perfectionist traits but there are many ways parents can help. It is helpful to explain that striving for excellence is a quest for reaching potential not perfection. Potential is about inner achievement such as being creative, taking risks, making new discoveries and thinking skills. This is far more important than high grades and awards. Show children that you value them more for who they are, not what they do and help them embrace that mistakes are part of learning. Encourage them to understand that achievement happens in incremental steps over time. Intelligence is not fixed. Struggling with a problem and practicing an activity actually builds brain cells.

It can be useful to tell them stories of famous people that illustrate some of these ideas. For example, Einstein failed botany, zoology and language in the polytechnic entrance exam, and it took him 20 attempts at theories before he came to his famous theory of relativity.

Edison stated that, "Genius is 1% inspiration and 99% perspiration."

Remember that mistakes are not failures. Mistakes can even become great successes. Penicillin was discovered by a scientist who accidently forgot to clean up his lab. In fact, 'Slinkys', mauve colour dye, the microwave oven and modern pacemakers (they used to be the size of a TV set) were all discovered through mistakes.

As a parent, you have great power to help your child tame their perfectionism. Try to involve children in fun activities where the aim is about the process and not the product (e.g., sculpture and art activities, collaborative games like 'Forbidden Island', 'Rory's Story Cubes',

'Concept' and 'Hanabi'). Model to your child that you're willing to attempt an activity in which you are incompetent and show that you can still enjoy the process. My children often collapse on the floor in the grip of hysterical laughter when I try and draw with them. My drawings of a 'brain' resemble 'sheep' and 'clouds' and mostly my artwork devolves to rudimentary stick figures! My inept attempts at drawing are certainly not 'perfect' but they do seem to make us all laugh. Proving that the process and adventure is much more important than the end result!

Chapter Nineteen
The Super Child

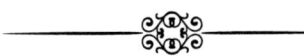

Who would have thought that World War III could have erupted over socks! Family life ignited! The culprit? One sock which felt itchy, too loose, not tight enough, wrong shade of white! Yes, my daughter could add up Yahtzee dice quicker than us at the age of four and was a philosopher about friendships at the age of five but none of that saved our world when socks were involved, and the intense trauma of hair rituals brought us close to cataclysm!

This is the world of a family with a gifted child. It was, and still is, a battle for her to embrace her quirkiness in a world where survival is to exist in a paradox – to be the same but different – but not too different – but also be yourself?

The high emotional energy and physical energy levels of a gifted child can't be ignored because they disturb routine and order. Hopefully to make a better, richer world despite the chaos that explodes in the interim. I recall my daughter continuously cartwheeling her way through a major shopping centre for two hours – narrowly missing the infirm and elderly while well-meaning onlookers encouraged her gymnastics prowess. As a parent, I was torn between admiring her co-ordination, energy and joy, and being terrified of the consequences of her actions. The task was harnessing this energy in a nurturing way without suffocating her spirit.

The current 'Yoda' in the clinical world of gifted children is Dabrowski, a Polish Psychiatrist. His theory was 'positive disintegration'. Rather than seeing development through linear age-related life stages he saw it as multidimensional. Human development is driven by reflection, self-evaluation and an urge for inner transformation. Dabrowski's 'Disintegration' is a way of dismantling thoughts to see and feel in a different way creating change and growth. Like a complex jigsaw that can be rearranged and seen from a different angle to create a new picture. The challenge for parents is being able to emotionally 'hold' the child while they are reconstructing so that their world (and the parent's) is not attacked by sharp jigsaw shards!

Giftedness can come in many different forms such as academic success, artistic pursuits, musical endeavours and in emotional awareness. Intelligence may not be directly observable in a rigid education system. The school system often misunderstands a gifted child as naughty, hyperactive and oppositional.

Along with giftedness comes overexcitabilities (Dabrowski) and this is where gifted children often collide with parents and society. There are five forms-psychomotor, sensual, intellectual, imaginational and emotional. It is the innate tendency to respond intensely to both external and internal stimuli. It creates a fervent aliveness.

Signs of Overexcitabilities
- Very high energy
- Strong reaction to sounds and smells.
- Rich fantasy life.
- Extremely curious, asks lots of questions.
- Seems to emotionally "overreact".

Strategies to cope with Overexcitabilities
- Routine and structure.
- Make time for physical activity and creative expression.
- Educate your child and significant others (siblings, teachers) about overexcitabilities.
- Encourage your child and others to see that overexcitabilities, when tamed, are a positive attribute (like a superpower).
- Teach your child to manage their intensity e.g., breathing, visualisation.
- Emphasis that being different is a positive and that everyone is 'quirky' in some way. Regularly tell them that you love and admire their difference and energy!

All humans have the capacity to push the human race forward. Gifted kids have extra spark. Maybe they have to be 'crazy'. How else can you stare at an empty page and see an epic story or work of art? Or gaze at a planet and imagine a universe? There is genius in this 'crazy' and 'crazy' can be tamed. Remember, the ones who are 'crazy' enough to think that they can change the world, are the ones who do.

Chapter Twenty
Are Children Growing Up Too Fast?

It seems to me that over the last decade, the adult world is insidiously encroaching on the world of children. The time when I innocently took my, then, 5-year-old daughter to the toilet at Miranda Fair Shopping Centre only to be confronted by her sounding out "H..E..R..P..E..S" which was written on the toilet door is firmly embedded in my memory. (She was very excited about her new prowess in reading!) It was a colourful ad for herpes treatment which any child would have found very attractive. Of course, the next words to come out of my tender, young child's mouth was "Mum, what's Herpes?" I was not quite prepared for this line of questioning ("Mum, what's a rainbow or a unicorn?" was more in my repertoire!) but I fumbled my way through and whatever l said seemed to satisfy her curiosity. I began to notice other strange anomalies. For instance, the "family" part of the video shop seemed to covertly gather PG and even M-rated movies. At first, subtly scattered amongst the shelves but later littered the shelves with flagrant disregard for the "family" sign above. The demise of video/DVD stores and rise of streaming on various electronic platforms (computers/TV) continues the trend of inappropriate rating systems.

What struck me as really scary was observing the emergence of "Lingerie Barbie" and a "Crystal Meth Lab Toy Lego Kit!" Only a few years ago, little girl underwear

with "eye candy" and "who needs credit cards" written on the crotch were removed from department stores. Although it was reassuring that the merchandise was withdrawn, it's very, very concerning that it made it through design, manufacture and production before it caused outrage. Were consumers supposed to think that they were just part of the "exciting range of choices" available? The exposure of children to inappropriate adult concepts has repercussions. Many factors contribute to unhealthy body image, low self-esteem, anxiety and depression but early exposure to sexualised images increases the risk.

A 2014 study by the Australian Institute of Family Studies revealed that children as young as 8 years old are dissatisfied with their body size and the majority of 10 to 11-year-olds are trying to control their weight. Girls as young as 5 years old believe that they are "ugly and fat". One in five girls suffers, to some degree, from anxiety manifesting as self-harm, eating disorders, binge drinking, bullying and risky sex. Boys are not immune from this over-sexualised culture. Consider the superhero costumes that are padded up to make 6-year-olds look like they have six-packs. I frequently see these boys frantically pushing themselves to do huge numbers of push-ups in an attempt to develop "super-abs" and not be taunted by school peers for being "weak" or "gay". Media and society encourage boys at an early age to be "macho" and "strong". The pressure to "man up" can lead to crash diets, overexercising and other dangerous behaviour. Sexualised media give boys a distorted and shallow view of girls and women and of their own masculinity. Our culture continues to discourage boys from talking about their feelings which leaves them isolated in their battle with anxiety and depression. These emotions often become expressed through defiant, aggressive behaviour.

The sexualisation of children is a community issue that requires response from parents as well as media, retailers and legislators. The pressure to achieve, behave and consume like adults at an early age is deadening childhood. The excitement for a girl of getting her first bra at twelve is stolen when she's been wearing a bra since she was 5 years old!

It is quite natural for little girls to play at imitating adults in their world but what is often projected through the media is adults playing "dress-up" with little girls for commercial purposes, not little girls playing "dress-up". Increasingly, rather than enjoying being a child, children are focussing too heavily on becoming what is perceived as a "successful" adult.

There is a great deal that you can do as a parent.

- Value your child for who they are and what they do. Not for their appearance.
- Emphasise health over looks.
- Keep children active.
- Be a role model by being healthy and positive about your own body.
- Be watchful of their social networks, texts, and online activity.
- Talk and listen to your children about how they feel about their body. Aim to have many conversations with them about why you may feel certain clothing and foods

are inappropriate.
- Encourage age-appropriate boundaries, activities and behaviour and play with your children.
- Discuss media and advertising messages with your children and encourage critical thinking.
- Listen to their ideas and explain your own thoughts.
- Reality check by explaining that famous people in glossy magazines are often photoshopped and that the image on the paper is an illusion. People do not look like that in real life.
- Talk to other parents and members of the community who can reinforce your perspective regarding age-appropriate issues.

If we can hold in mind Einstein's wisdom that "the world is a dangerous place, not because of those who do evil but because of those who look on and do nothing", we do have the power to pave a safer, brighter path for our children.

Chapter Twenty-One
Epilogue

You never really stop being a parent.

"Affirming words from mums and dads are like light switches. Speak a word of affirmation at the right moment in a child's life and it's like lighting up a whole roomful of possibilities." – Gary Smalley, family therapist.

It really doesn't matter how old you or your child is – you never stop being a parent. My 92-year-old great aunt (my adopted mother) never stops worrying and caring about me and my children. She also continues to be ecstatic to hear of our adventures and proud of our achievements. When I recently told her that my daughter had received an offer to go to the University of Sydney (a relatively prestigious university) she was exhilarated and proud. She gleefully exclaimed that she could hardly breathe with happiness (a bit concerning for us given she is 92 years old) and that this fantastic news had made her day! Ten minutes later the phone rang again. The glee had twisted to anxiety and terror as she realised that my daughter would have to travel on her own by public transport into the city. This joy and adjoining terror portray an interesting mix of emotion that many parents experience.

The aspiration held in this book is that it gives parents hope and clues to understand and enjoy their children, even during some taxing situations. Some of the universally common elements of parenthood such as confusion, frustration, laughter and joy are highlighted in a way to illuminate to parents that they are not alone. All parents are somewhat lost at sea (as are all humans really), every now and then landing on small islands of rest and contentment before being flung back adrift into the ocean again. Catching glimpses of the sun and stars to find their way and sometimes finding amazing wise people and creatures who advise and encourage them to trust their instincts.

Having some understanding of the meaning behind children's behaviour also helps parents to navigate the bumps along the journey and take detours to avoid collisions. Sometimes the only successful way through, is to forge determinedly over the bump and weather the storm to get to the other side, hopefully to calmer moments.

The ability to see the humour in difficult situations is one of the essential ingredients in resilience, and it is also something that you can pass onto your children, by modelling to them how you deal with stressful situations. Being a parent is the most important job in the world, the hardest job in the world but also the most enriching, awesome job in the world!